AF582122

This book belongs to:

To my grandfather Leonardo, to the ones have left us, and to all grandparents who are still sharing their experiences and family values with those they love.

Original Title in Spanish: Mi abuelo y yo nos parecemos

Edited by: Dr. Renea Skelton.

Published By: Monarchbm Publishing .

For permissions requests, contact publisher at:
permissionrequests@monarchbmp.com

ISBN 979-8-9855945-5-3

My grandpa and I look like each other.
He lost three teeth and so did I.

He was sad but I was happy because Mr. Mouse brought me five dollars! Later, when my grandpa went to the dentist to fix his teeth, he was happy again.

My grandpa loves walking in nature, talking to farm animals, and taking care of the trees. He lives in the country surrounded by natural beauties like lakes, mountains, trees, and a beautiful light blue sky.

I also like nature and enjoy exploring it running around from place to place. But my grandpa walks slowly, and I walk fast. I live in the United States and my grandpa lives in Mexico. I love the nature and the village where my grandpa lives.

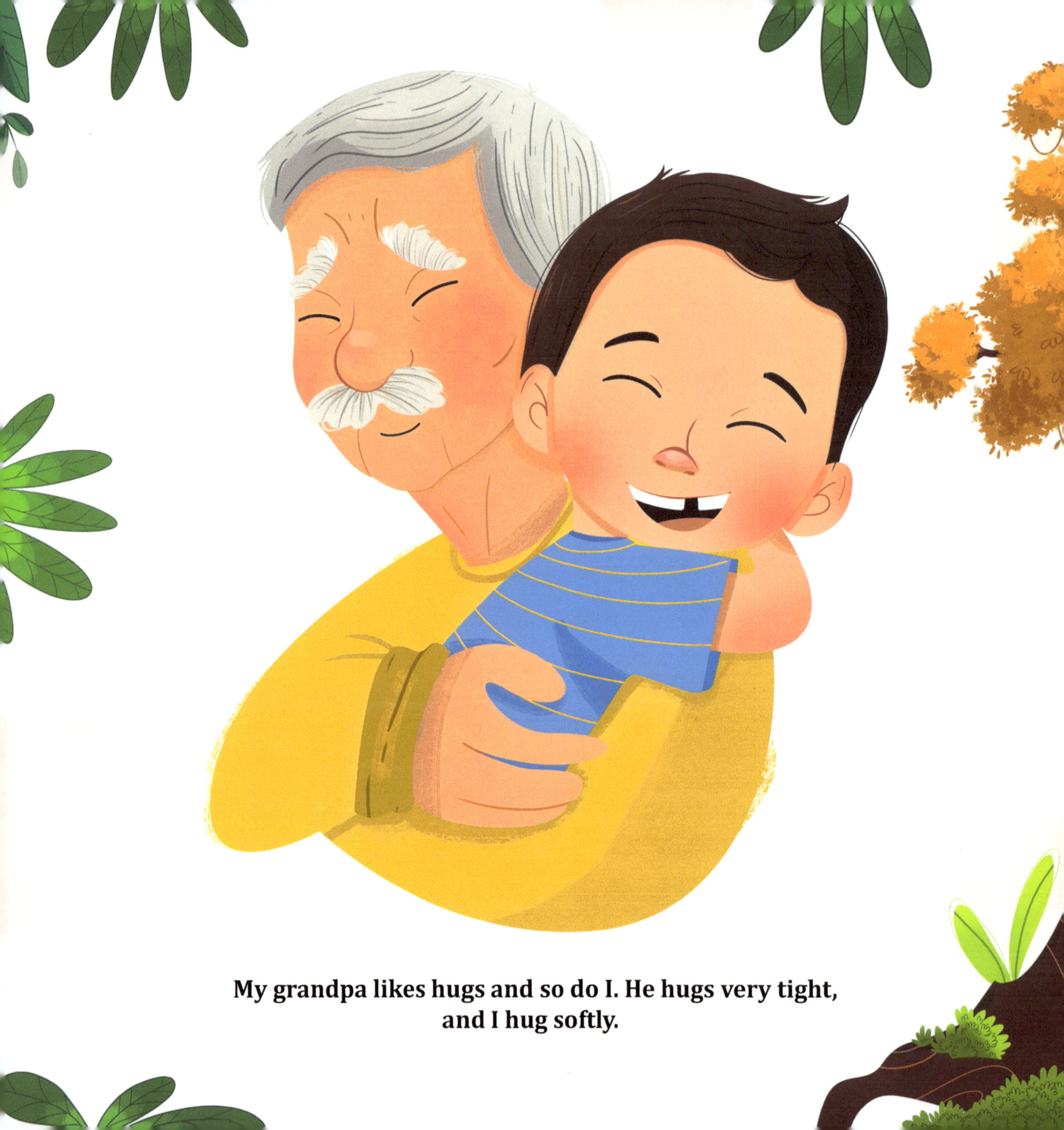

My grandpa likes hugs and so do I. He hugs very tight, and I hug softly.

When I arrive at his house, I jump
in his arms and give him a big hug.
I almost make him fall over!

My grandpa likes to have lots of friends
and enjoys spending time with them.
But he has only one friend left.

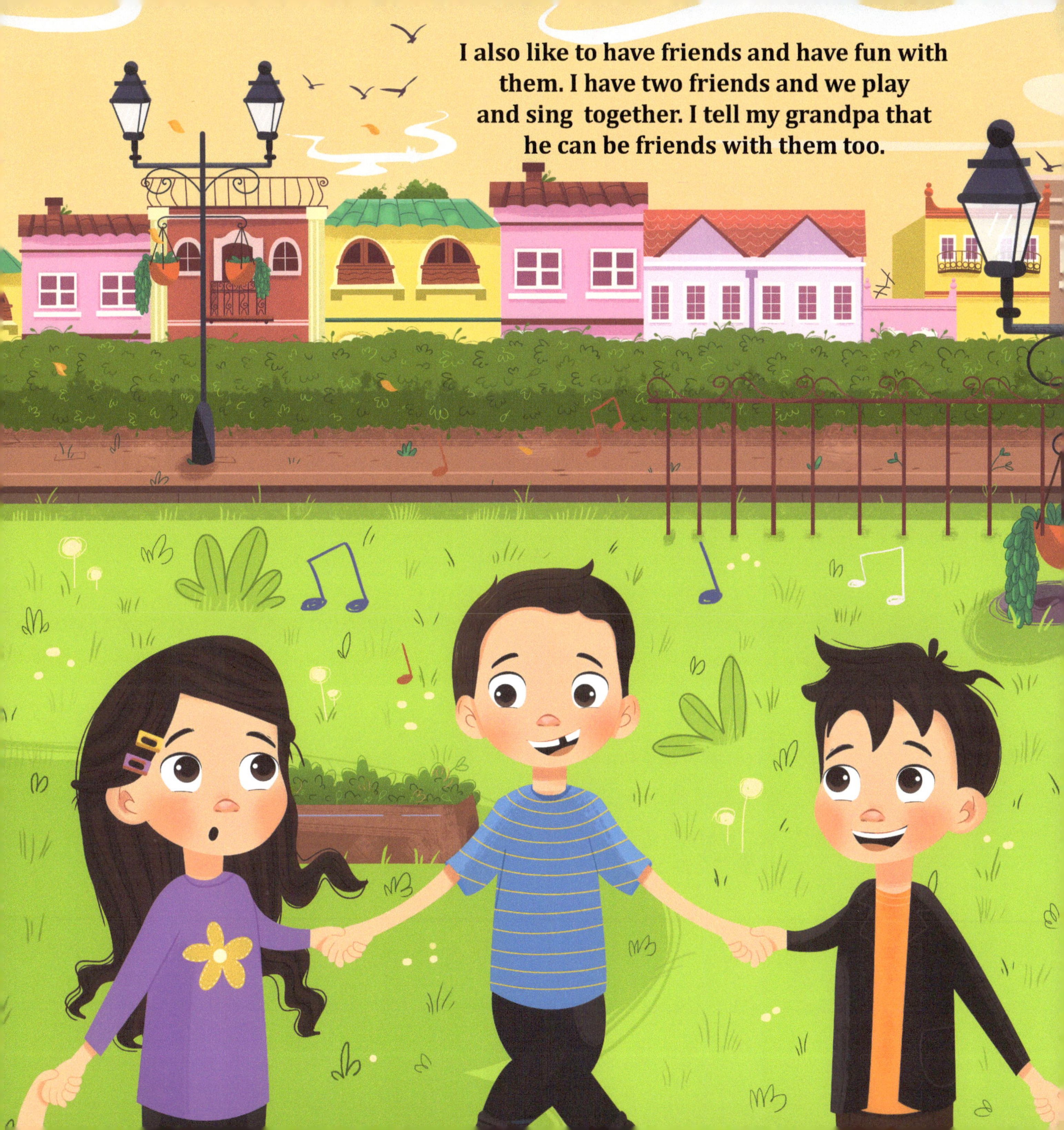

I also like to have friends and have fun with them. I have two friends and we play and sing together. I tell my grandpa that he can be friends with them too.

Sometimes, my grandpa does not like the food that grandma cooks for him. He says it's salty and has a little bit of fat.

I don't like to eat some of the veggies my mom prepares for me either, I tell her they need salt. Secretly, I love carrots and broccoli because they are very tasty.

When we go to the park,
my grandpa gets on the swing
and swings slowly. The wind
pushes him forward
very gently.

When I get on the swing, I go so fast and
imagine that I'm flying in the air.

Sometimes, my grandpa silently cries when he misses his children or when he loses a friend.

I also cry, but loudly, when I miss my parents, my cousins, or when I have to say goodbye to relatives after visiting them.

My grandpa needs to be taken to the doctor often for his regular checkups and to receive his shots. He is very brave and does not scream when he gets them.

I also need to be taken to the doctor often
for my shots. I am not that brave and shout out loud,
"Aweeeeee!"

My grandpa always goes to bed early. When the sun goes down, he feels tired and goes to his room to sleep.

I also must go to bed early even if I'm not tired and feel lots of energy. I start jumping up and down on the bed before I fall asleep. I do this without my mom knowing.

Early in the morning, as soon as the rooster sings and the sun rises, my grandpa gets up and goes outside to see the beautiful sunrise. I can hear the barking dogs, the chirping birds, the chicken's cluck, the bleating of the sheep, and the horses' neighs. There's also a beautiful pond by my grandpa's house where the ducks chatter in the water.

As soon as I hear the rooster crowing, I quickly get up, put on my shoes, and go outside to enjoy the beautiful day. I'm so excited and greet all the farm animals by their names. Polar and Lila are puppies, and are just waking up!

My grandpa loves to read and write. He writes a lot about his life and has hundreds of adventures to share. He was a great leader in his village. The government wanted to take away people's houses, but my grandpa made it possible for them to feel safe and to own their own land. Many schools were built, and trees were planted because of him.

I also like to read and write. I often write about my daily adventures such as, "My adventures with the hen that chased me for playing with its chicks."

My grandpa loves ice cream. Near his village, there's a small town called Dolores de Colores. It's a very historic and colorful place. You can find all kinds of ice cream that you could possibly imagine. They even have odd flavors like zapote (which is an exotic fruit), pork cracklings, shrimp, and cheese. Believe it or not they are very tasty!

I love ice cream too. My grandpa gets a zapote flavor and I get strawberry with lime. It’s delicious!

Sometimes, my grandpa doesn't hear very well, and we need to repeat the words, especially when we tell him it's time for his shower.

Sometimes, I can't hear very well either, especially when my mom tells me it's bath time and I need to stop playing. Hmmm, I wonder why...!

Don't you think it's amazing that my grandpa is 81 and I'm only 6 years old and we still have fun together? The other day, I fell asleep when he was telling me a story about the Mexican Revolution. I love his stories!

My grandpa and I have lots of things in common. We easily express our feelings; we like to receive love and we need somebody to take care of us and treat us well. But we also are responsible, respectful, and cheerful to the people around us. The funny thing is that, even when we are toothless, we laugh out loud, showing all our teeth or what little we have!

Although, there is only one small thing my grandpa doesn't like and that's stuffed animals. One day I made him laugh so much, because I told him to "hug my stuffed animal, grandpa!" He crunched himself up while laughing and said, "No, no I don't like stuffed animals." It was so fun seeing him laugh.

When I visit my grandparents, I always have a wonderful experience, and spending time with my grandpa made me realize that I'm just like him!

If you have grandparents, take care of them. Give them lots of love, hugs, and make them laugh. You can even give them a kiss or a smile to express your love.

It's possible that one day you will be a grandpa or grandma and will spend time and share stories with your grandchildren. You may even find out that even though you're different, you are a lot alike!

www.ingramcontent.com/pod-product-compliance
Lightning Source LLC
LaVergne TN
LVHW071217160826
845679LV00003B/857

* 9 7 9 8 9 8 5 5 9 4 5 5 3 *